# GLOSSARY

**Astronaut** A person who has been trained to travel in space.

**Space Probe** A spacecraft for exploring space and other planets. It is controlled by computers back on Earth.

**Orbit** The oval-shaped movement of a planet or moon around a star or another planet.

**Spacecraft** A vehicle that can travel in space.

**Ignite** To make something burn or heat up strongly.

In the far future, we may be able to use rockets to travel to other stars in the galaxy and even settle on other Earth-like planets! Stay tuned, space explorers. Maybe you will have your own rocket someday! Until then, keep looking toward the stars.

# ROCKETS FOR ALL!

Soon, ordinary people may be able to travel on rockets! Many people are designing rockets for space tourism. Imagine having your summer vacation on the moon or even on Mars!

Orion will be able to carry astronauts to Mars and beyond. This is much further than any spacecraft has ever gone!

# OUR NEXT MISSION: TO MARS AND BEYOND

We don't use space shuttles anymore. Scientists are working on a new spacecraft called Orion.

ORION

Orion will use newer, better rockets called the Space Launch System. They will be the most powerful rockets ever built!

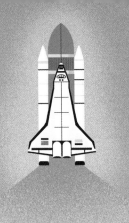

Challenger had nine successful missions.
It carried the first American woman,
Sally Ride, and the first African American
person, Guion Bluford, into space!

# GREAT SHUTTLES AND THEIR MISSIONS

This is Columbia. It was the first space shuttle to go into space and land back on Earth. It ran 27 successful missions!

Here is Discovery. It carried the Hubble Space Telescope, which let us take pictures of very distant stars and planets!

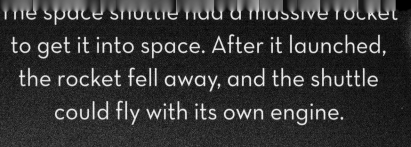

The space shuttle had a massive rocket to get it into space. After it launched, the rocket fell away, and the shuttle could fly with its own engine.

Space shuttles could orbit around Earth and then land just like airplanes. One space shuttle could be used many times, as long as it had a new rocket for every launch!

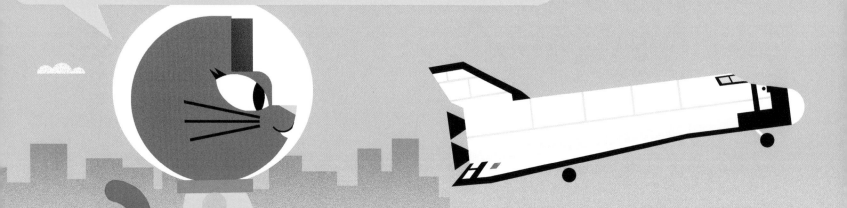

# MODERN SPACE SHUTTLES

Around 10 years after Apollo 11, scientists created a new kind of spacecraft: a space shuttle.

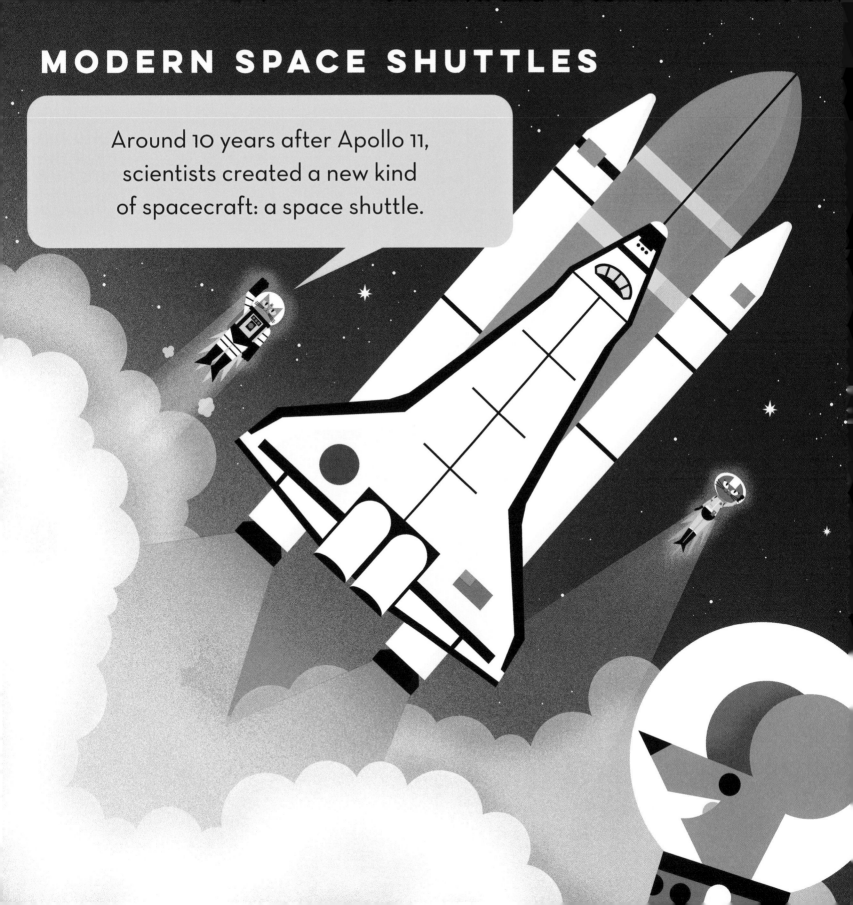

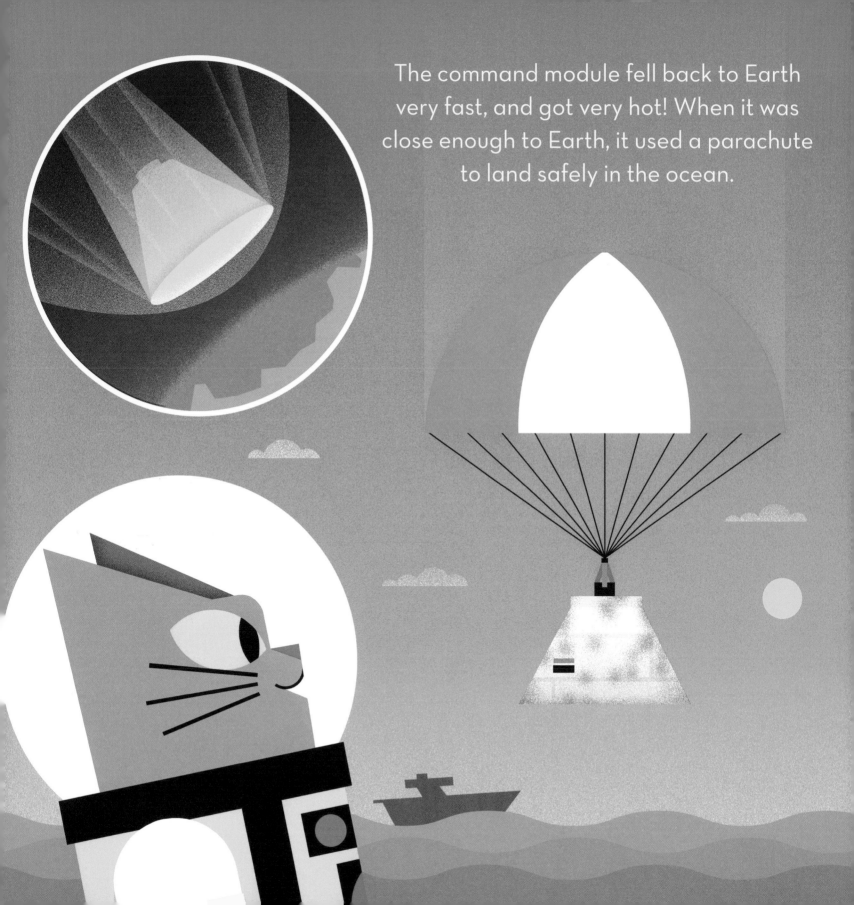

The command module fell back to Earth very fast, and got very hot! When it was close enough to Earth, it used a parachute to land safely in the ocean.

# GETTING BACK TO EARTH

**LUNAR MODULE**

**APOLLO 11**

Once all three astronauts were back on Apollo 11, the lunar module was left to float away.

Finally, the last rocket engine broke off and floated away, as it was no longer needed.

All that was left was this small part, the command module.

When they were done, the lunar module's small rocket engines launched them back into space to rejoin the command module.

# LANDING ON THE MOON

Astronauts on Apollo 11 used the lunar module to land on the moon. It was a small vehicle that could separate itself from the spacecraft.

Two astronauts landed on the moon, while the third stayed in the spacecraft. They collected rocks to bring back for scientists to study.

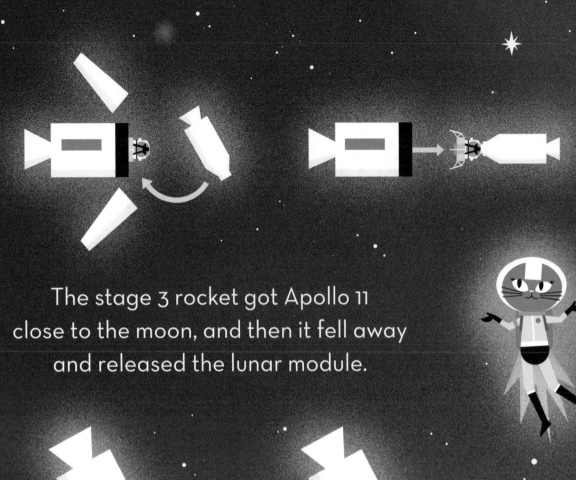

The stage 3 rocket got Apollo 11
close to the moon, and then it fell away
and released the lunar module.

# STAGES OF THE LAUNCH

This is the stage 1 rocket. It got
Apollo 11 off the ground and into space.
Once it had no fuel left, it broke away.

Then, the stage 2 rocket
**ignited** and pushed further into
space. Then it fell away too.

# APOLLO 11

Here is the Apollo 11 capsule. In the year 1969, it carried the first humans to ever walk on the moon.

After that, scientists began to send other animals into space. Some of the first were a dog named Laika and a monkey named Albert.

In 1961, a Russian man named Yuri Gagarin became the first person to travel in space. He went around the Earth once on a rocket.

# HISTORY OF SPACE TRAVEL

In 1947, the first living beings were sent into space. It wasn't safe for people yet, so instead they sent fruit flies.

A similar thing happens if you let go of a balloon that has air inside. The air rushes out of it, making it fly around!

# ROCKETS

A rocket's engine is like a car's, except that it burns a lot more fuel and it is much hotter!

When the rocket fuel burns, it pushes out hot gas. The gas moves so fast toward the ground that it pushes the rocket upwards.

We need to use a special vehicle with a huge amount of energy to beat the powerful pull of gravity. This vehicle is called a rocket.

# HOW DO YOU GET TO SPACE?

First we need to leave Earth. We can't just jump into the air and float into space, because gravity is very strong.

Gravity is the force that pulls everything toward the Earth. When you jump up and then fall back down, this is gravity at work!

In order to learn about space, we send **astronauts** or **space probes** to these places. Would you like to see? Let's go!

# TRAVELING THROUGH SPACE

When you look up at the sky at night, you are actually looking into outer space. How cool is that?

All of those tiny lights are stars and planets that are millions of miles away. If we got closer, we would see that they are actually very big. Many are even bigger than planet Earth.

PROFESSOR ASTRO CAT'S
# SPACE ROCKETS
## DR. DOMINIC WALLIMAN & BEN NEWMAN

•FLYING EYE BOOKS•
LONDON | NEW YORK

To my very special friends,
Nick White and Laura Beckett.

— BN

*Professor Astro Cat's Space Rockets* © Flying Eye Books 2018.

This is a first edition published in 2018 by Flying Eye Books, an imprint
of Nobrow Ltd. 27 Westgate Street, London E8 3RL.

Illustrations by Ben Newman. Text by Dominic Walliman and Avalon Nuovo.

Dominic Walliman and Ben Newman have asserted their right under the Copyright,
Designs and Patents Act, 1988, to be identified as the Author and Illustrator of this Work.

Published in the US by Nobrow (US) Inc.

Printed in Latvia on FSC® certified paper.

ISBN: 978-1-911171-94-2

Order from www.flyingeyebooks.com

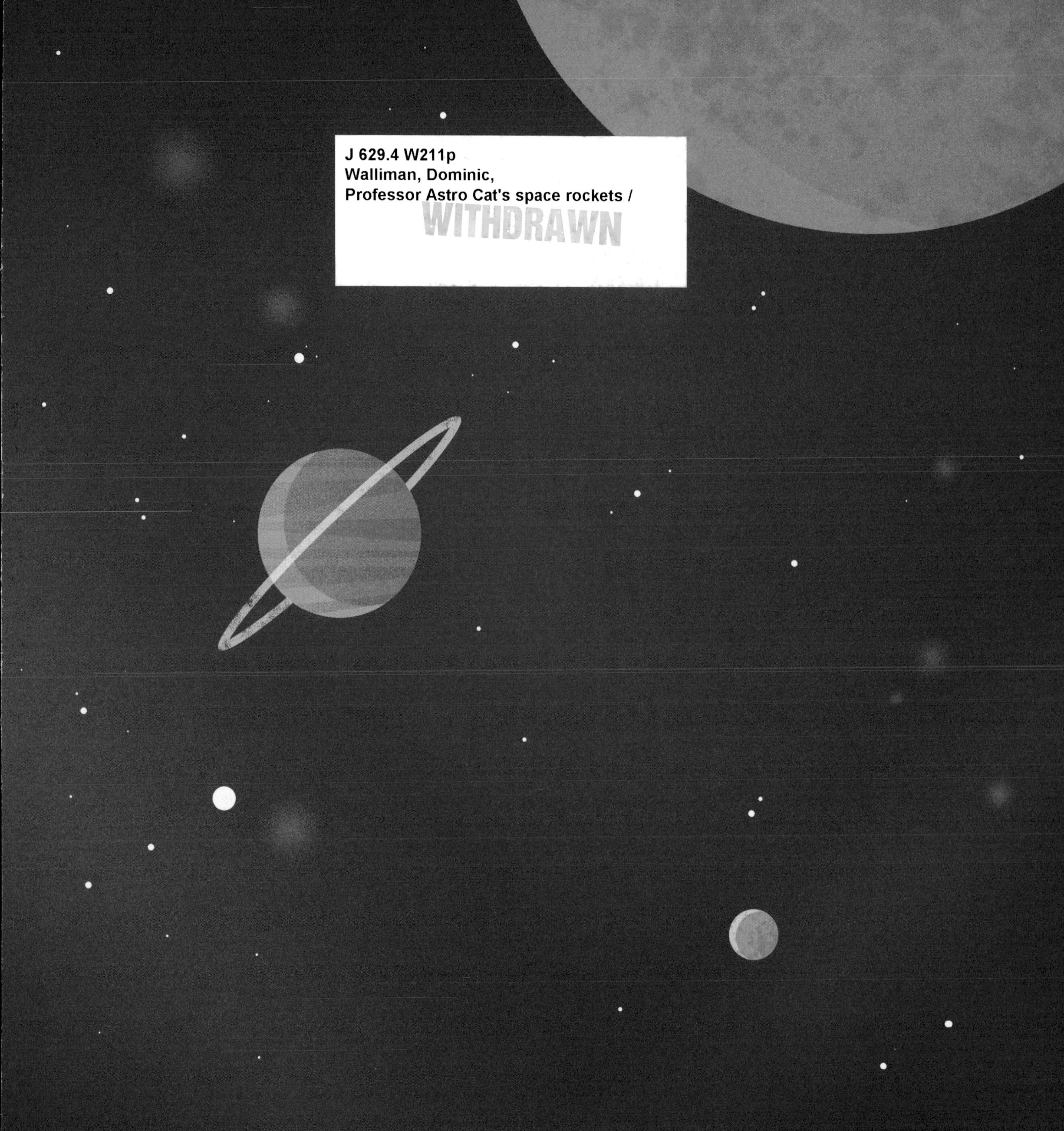